GLOBALHOTSPOTS

SUDAN

Geoff Barker

Marshall Cavendish
Benchmark
New York

This edition first published in 2009 in the United States of America by
Marshall Cavendish Benchmark.

Marshall Cavendish Benchmark
99 White Plains Road
Tarrytown, NY 10591
www.marshallcavendish.us

All Internet sites were available and accurate when sent to press.

First published in 2008 by
MACMILLAN EDUCATION AUSTRALIA PTY LTD
15–19 Claremont Street, South Yarra 3141

Visit our website at www.macmillan.com.au or go directly to www.macmillanlibrary.com.au

Associated companies and representatives throughout the world.

Copyright © Macmillan Education Australia 2008

Barker, Geoff.
    Sudan / by Geoff Barker.
    p. cm. –(Global hotspots)
    Includes index.
    ISBN 978-0-7614-3182-4
    1.Sudan–Juvenile literature.I. Title.
    DT154.6.B37 2008
    962.4–dc22

2008018688

Produced for Macmillan Education Australia by
MONKEY PUZZLE MEDIA LTD
The Rectory, Eyke, Woodbridge, Suffolk IP12 2QW, UK

Edited by Susie Brooks
Text and cover design by Tom Morris and James Winrow
Page layout by Tom Morris
Photo research by Lynda Lines
Maps by Martin Darlison, Encompass Graphics

Printed in the United States

Acknowledgments
The author and the publisher are grateful to the following for permission to reproduce copyright material:

Front cover photograph: Refugees at a Red Crescent hospital in Nyala, Darfur, 2007. Courtesy of Getty Images (AFP).

Corbis, pp. **4** (Nic Bothma/epa), **7** (Michael Freeman), **11** (Bettmann), **12** (Bettmann), **13** (Bettmann), **14** (Bettmann), **15** (Bettmann), **21** (Reuters), **22** (UNICEF/Georgina Cransto/epa), **23** (Thomas Mukoya/Reuters), **26** (Lynsey Addario), **27** (Richard Wainwright), **28** (Lynsey Addario); Getty Images, pp. **6** (AFP), **8** (Hulton Archive), **9** (George William Joy), **10** (Robert George Talbot Kelly), **16** (Hulton Archive), **17** (National Geographic), **18, 19, 20** (Time & Life Pictures), **25** (AFP), **29**; iStockphoto, p. **30**.

While every care has been taken to trace and acknowledge copyright, the publisher tenders their apologies for any accidental infringement where copyright has proved untraceable. Where the attempt has been unsuccessful, the publisher welcomes information that would redress the situation.

1 3 5 6 4 2

CONTENTS

Glossary words

When a word is printed in **bold**, you can look
up its meaning in the Glossary on page 31.

ALWAYS IN THE NEWS

Global hot spots are places that are always in the news. They are places where there has been conflict between different groups of people for years. Sometimes the conflicts have lasted for hundreds of years.

Why Do Hot Spots Happen?

There are four main reasons why hot spots happen:

1 Disputes over land, and who has the right to live on it.

2 Disagreements over religion and **culture**, where different peoples find it impossible to live happily side-by-side.

3 Arguments over how the government should be organized.

4 Conflict over resources, such as oil, gold, or diamonds.

Sometimes these disagreements spill over into violence—and into the headlines.

Conflict in Sudan has left millions of people homeless and in need of foreign aid. These Sudanese families are waiting to receive help from a French aid organization.

Sudan

Sudan is a large country in the north part of Africa. Darfur is in western Sudan and it hit the headlines in 2003 when violence erupted. Villages were burned and thousands of people were murdered. But Sudan's problems did not begin then. Sudan was already a hot spot.

After Fifty Years of Civil War

In 2003, Sudan had already suffered nearly fifty years of **civil war** between the north and the south. People in northern Sudan are mainly Muslim. Those in the south are non-Muslim. The southern Sudanese disliked the way that the government in Khartoum, the **capital city** in the north, made decisions for the whole country.

HOT SPOT BRIEFING

COUNTRY NAME
The name Sudan means "land of the black people."

Sudan is bordered by nine other countries and the Red Sea.

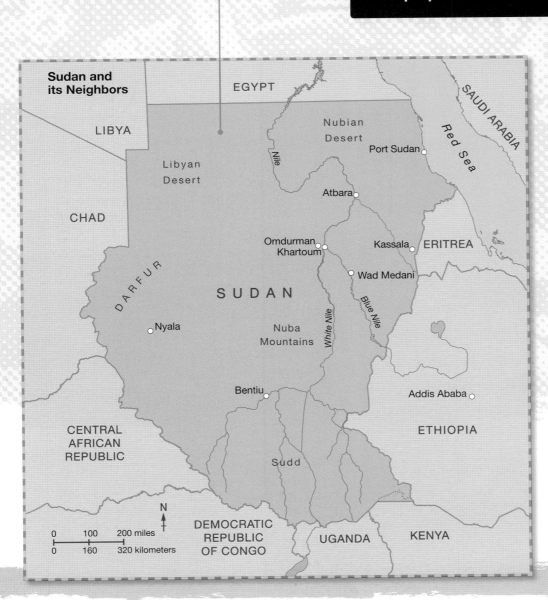

Sudan and its Neighbors

EGYPT

LIBYA

Nubian Desert

Red Sea

SAUDI ARABIA

Port Sudan

Libyan Desert

Nile

Atbara

CHAD

Omdurman
Khartoum

Kassala

ERITREA

Wad Medani

DARFUR

S U D A N

Blue Nile

White Nile

Nyala

Nuba Mountains

Bentiu

Addis Ababa

CENTRAL AFRICAN REPUBLIC

Sudd

ETHIOPIA

N

0   100   200 miles
0   160   320 kilometers

DEMOCRATIC REPUBLIC OF CONGO

UGANDA   KENYA

A DIVIDED NATION

For most of its early history, Sudan was made up of smaller, independent kingdoms. Ancient divisions, including differences in religion and culture, have divided the nation. These divisions are at the root of the conflicts in recent years.

Christianity and Islam

One of Sudan's most important ancient kingdoms was Nubia, in northern Sudan. During the 500s CE, Egyptian **missionaries** traveled to Nubia and converted the people to Christianity. Then, in the mid-600s, Arab Muslims from Egypt began to trade and settle in the region. They married local Nubian women. The religion of Islam began to spread.

HOT SPOT BRIEFING

ISLAM
Islam is a religion founded by the Arab **prophet** Mohammed in the 600s CE. Followers of Islam are Muslims. They worship one god, called Allah.

A Sudanese Muslim threads prayer beads outside a mosque in Khartoum. Mosques are Muslim places of worship.

Northern Peoples

Arab religious leaders gradually converted the northern kingdoms to Islam. Today, northern Sudan has a mainly Arab population as well as a Nubian population. Nubians are non-Arab Muslims.

Southern Peoples

By the 1500s, black African groups from other parts of the continent began to settle in the south of Sudan. These groups, such as the Dinka, Nuer, and Shilluk, have various traditional African or Christian beliefs. They still make up most of the southern Sudanese population.

Cattle stroll through a Dinka camp in southern Sudan. The Dinka are nomads, moving from place to place to find grazing for their animals.

SUDAN

Sudan is the largest country in Africa and is just over one-quarter the size of the United States. Sudan is a divided country of twenty-six states. There are about 175 different major tribes, or groups, and another 325 smaller ones.

HOT SPOT BRIEFING

TRADITIONAL AFRICAN BELIEFS
There are many traditional African beliefs among the people of southern Sudan. These vary from group to group. Many believe there is one creator, or god. The Dinkas worship one god whom they call Nhialic. Other Dinkas are Christian.

REBELLION AGAINST THE EGYPTIANS

Throughout history, Sudan has been strongly influenced by Egypt, its northern neighbor. By the early 1800s, Egypt controlled most of Sudan. In 1821, a new Egyptian government called the Turkiyah was in place in Khartoum.

Muhammad Ahmed, or the Mahdi, was born in 1848. He died in 1885, shortly after defeating the Egyptians.

The Turkiyah and the Mahdi

The Turkiyah ruled northern Sudan, but they tended not to listen to the needs of the southern Sudanese. Their unsympathetic rule made them unpopular across most of the country. In 1881, a Sudanese Muslim called the Mahdi led a revolt against the Egyptians. Many Sudanese groups united with him to fight against the foreign rule.

HOT SPOT BRIEFING

THE MAHDI
Muhammad Ahmed was a Muslim religious teacher. He was known mainly as the Mahdi, or "expected one." This meant that he thought he was the second great religious prophet, after Mohammed, who was the founder of Islam.

The Mahdi's Revolt

The Mahdi's revolt was successful. The Egyptians did not have a very strong army and had to ask the foreign power of Britain for help. Britain sent forces led by General Charles Gordon to help defend Khartoum. The Mahdi's rebels killed Gordon and captured Khartoum. In 1885, Sudan announced its independence from Egypt. The Mahdi set up a new government, called the Mahdiyyah.

"[the Mahdi] put life and soul into the hearts of his countrymen and freed his native land of foreigners."

British historian and politician Winston Churchill in his book, *The River War* (1899).

General Gordon's Last Stand, by British artist George William Joy. This painting shows the moments before the death of General Charles Gordon (standing top left).

EGYPTIAN AND BRITISH CONTROL

The Egyptians and British soon joined forces to fight against Sudan again. In 1898, the armies met at the Battle of Omdurman, near Khartoum. The Sudanese had far greater numbers, but they faced the modern weapons of the combined British and Egyptian forces.

Sudan Loses the Battle

In 1898, the leader of Sudan and successor to the Mahdi was Khalifa Abdullah. He and his Sudanese soldiers lacked modern weapons. Their swords and rifles were defeated by the cannons and machine guns used by Britain and Egypt.

WAR CASUALTIES

STATISTICS

The Battle of Omdurman was never an equal contest. Fewer than fifty British and Egyptian soldiers died. Sudan lost as many as 10,000 men during the battle.

The Flight of the Khalifa after his Defeat at the Battle of Omdurman, by British artist Robert George Talbot Kelly. Khalifa Abdullah is seen here retreating from the British and Egyptian forces in 1898.

Joint Rule of Sudan

Once again Sudan came under the control of the Egyptians. This time the country was ruled jointly by Britain and Egypt. It became known as Anglo-Egyptian Sudan. Sudanese people did help to run the country, but they were given mainly minor jobs.

Sudanese Begin to Rebel

Many Sudanese people began to protest against the foreign rule. In 1924, Sudanese troops rebelled against the British. The **mutiny** failed, but it showed how the Sudanese resented the British presence. This resentment lasted for many years.

Sudanese rioters in 1924 wave their flags in protest against the British, near the city of Atbara in northern Sudan.

INDEPENDENCE

In 1953, Britain and Egypt began a process to allow Sudan to govern itself. It would take three years before Sudan could finally become a fully independent country.

New Parliament

In 1954, the Sudanese people voted for a new **parliament**. Ismail al-Azhari of the National Unionist Party became the first prime minister of Sudan. On December 19, 1955 Sudan's parliament voted for complete independence for the country.

Officially Independent

On January 1, 1956, it became official. Sudan was finally an independent country. British and Egyptian troops left the region. A **constitution** was drawn up on how the country was to be run. However, independence did not bring an end to tensions between northern and southern Sudan.

HOT SPOT BRIEFING

CIVILIAN GOVERNMENT
Over the years, Sudan has had many military governments, but its first government was a **civilian** government. Arab leader Ismail al-Azhari ruled the country from the government's northern base, in Khartoum.

Ismail al-Azhari, seen here in 1954, served as prime minister of Sudan from 1954 to 1956. He became president in 1964 and served until 1969.

Independent but not United

In 1956, Sudan was independent but not united. Southern leaders did not trust the new government in Khartoum. They did not believe that the northern leaders would listen to their needs or share power equally with them.

In 1954, al-Azhari made a short visit to Egypt. He is seen here (left) with Egyptian leader Gamal Abdel Nasser (center), being greeted by local crowds.

FIRST CIVIL WAR

The first Sudanese government struggled to deal with the great divide between northern and southern Sudan. Tensions grew between the mainly Christian and African south and the Muslim north. Sudan's first civil war erupted.

Military Takeover

In 1958, Sudan was a country in crisis. A powerful Arab army officer, General Ibrahim Abboud, overthrew the government and set up military rule. He then tried to force the southern leaders to work with his new Arab government. This action only increased the tensions with people in the south.

Sudanese Workers Rebel

Abboud's military government was strict and unpopular. In 1964, Sudanese workers rebelled against it. The first protesters were students and teachers at the University of Khartoum. Then **civil servants** and others across the country stopped work and held a general strike. There was rioting. Eventually the workers forced the army to help overthrow Abboud. The Sudanese government was once again under civilian control.

Sudanese leader Ibrahim Abboud attends a meeting for African heads of state in 1963 in Ethiopia.

Military Power Once More

In May 1969, Muslim army officer Colonel Gaafar Nimeiri seized power. To make his position stronger, he banned political parties in Sudan and put many politicians in prison. In October 1970, his armed forces made a major attack on rebel camps in southern Sudan. However, Nimeiri also announced that he was willing to start talks with southern leaders, including an influential former army officer, General Joseph Lagu.

HOT SPOT BRIEFING

NIMEIRI UNDER PRESSURE
When Colonel Nimeiri came to power in 1969, the country was still unstable. Some members of Nimeiri's government saw their chance to take power for themselves. Nimeiri decided to act harshly and arrested them and many other leading politicians.

In 1969, Colonel Gaafar Nimeiri seized power in Sudan in what became known as the "May Revolution."

PEACE WITH THE SOUTH

In 1972, Sudanese leader Colonel Nimeiri made peace with southern rebels. He finally agreed that the non-Muslims of the south should be able to run their own part of the country.

End of Seventeen-Year Civil War

In March 1972, Colonel Nimeiri met with rebel leader General Joseph Lagu in Addis Ababa, Ethiopia, to sign a peace agreement. After seventeen years of civil war, fighting between northern and southern Sudan was finally over. Peace lasted for eleven years, until 1983.

A group of southern Sudanese villagers prepare a dance to celebrate peace in 1972.

Self-Government for the South

Under the peace agreement, Colonel Nimeiri granted southern Sudan a single regional government. The region was able to make its own laws, giving it a certain amount of self-government.

Oil!

In 1978, oil was discovered in Bentiu, southern Sudan. It was significant that this rich resource was found in the south. Oil became another important factor in the complex north–south conflict. The north wanted to keep the wealth that oil would bring. Sudan began exporting oil to other countries in 1999.

BARRELS OF OIL

By the end of 1998, Sudan was producing 18,000 to 20,000 barrels of oil a day. In September 1999, the first shipment of 600,000 barrels left Port Sudan.

An oil rig stands in the distance at Bentiu, southern Sudan. This woman sells tea to the oil workers.

SECOND CIVIL WAR

In 1983, Sudan's peace ended. Nimeiri made new Muslim laws for the whole country, which upset non-Muslims from the south. Civil war broke out again. This was the beginning of the end for Nimeiri, who was finally thrown from power in 1985.

Islamic Law for All

Nimeiri set up Islamic law across Sudan because he thought it was more important to have support from northern Muslims than southern Christians and Africans. In a further blow to the south, Nimeiri ended regional government in southern Sudan. Fighting broke out between northern government forces and the south.

HOT SPOT BRIEFING

SHARIA LAW

Islamic law is called Sharia. It is based on the Muslim holy book, the Qur'an, and other sacred texts. From 1983, lawbreakers in Sudan suddenly faced traditional Islamic punishments. This meant, for instance, that people caught with alcohol were beaten in public. Non-Muslims, including southerners, faced the same punishments as Muslims.

Southern fighters like these joined forces in 1983 and formed the Sudan People's Liberation Army (SPLA).

Leading the South

In 1983, a Dinka named John Garang became leader of the Sudan People's Liberation Army (SPLA). John Garang and his party were willing to fight for independence for the south. Their fight went on until 2004.

A New Islamic Leader

Brigadier-General Omar al-Bashir led a political party called the National Islamic Front (NIF). In 1989, with Sudan still weak from civil war, he and a group of military officers saw the chance to take power. Sudan was about to enter a new era.

Southern rebel leader John Garang poses for a portrait in 1992, as his fight for southern independence continues.

A BASE FOR TERRORISM

During the mid-1990s, Sudan and the United States began to become enemies. The main reason was that Sudan had become a base for Islamic **terrorist** groups. These included **al-Qaeda**, led by Osama bin Laden.

Islamic Terrorists

Al-Qaeda does not like to see foreign powers, particularly the United States, in Muslim countries. In the 1990s, American troops were based in the Muslim country of Saudi Arabia. Osama bin Laden, the leader of al-Qaeda, is a Saudi Arabian Muslim. In 1992, he moved to Sudan in order to run his terror campaign in hiding. Sudan's leader, Omar al-Bashir, welcomed him and offered al-Qaeda and other terrorists a safe **haven**.

The United States Attacks Sudan

The United States suspected that Sudan had links with al-Qaeda. In 1998, they launched a missile attack on a chemical plant in Sudan's capital city, Khartoum. Several Sudanese civilians died in the attack.

HOT SPOT BRIEFING

TERRORISTS IN SUDAN
Omar al-Bashir allowed members of al-Qaeda and other Islamic **extremist** groups to live and train in Sudan. In return, Sudan received money.

The al-Shifa chemical plant in Khartoum lies in ruins in 1998, after the American missile attack.

Terrorist attacks on the United States

Al-Qaeda's hatred toward the Americans grew. On September 11, 2001, al-Qaeda launched a series of air attacks on the United States. More than 3,000 people died. Later that year, the United States accused Sudan of being involved in international terrorism. Shortly after this, they made special **sanctions**, or restrictions, on Sudan.

In 2002, Omar al-Bashir (left) met with Ugandan President Museveni (right) and others, as part of a bid to improve relations between Sudan and the rest of the world.

Difficult Relations

In the early 2000s, Sudan's government faced major problems. Relations with the United States had become difficult because of Sudan's support of Islamic extremist groups. Meanwhile, in southern Sudan, rebels were uniting under the leadership of John Garang. Bashir's government needed to make peace both within and outside Sudan.

A NEW PEACE AGREEMENT

From 2002, Omar al-Bashir's government and John Garang's southern rebels started taking steps towards peace. After so many years of fighting, civil war was finally coming to an end.

First Step to Agreement

In July 2002, the Sudanese government and southern rebels signed the Machakos **Protocol**. In this draft treaty, the government agreed not to make southerners follow Islamic law. This was an important step toward ending the civil war. One week later, President Bashir and John Garang met for the first time.

TOLL OF THE SECOND CIVIL WAR

STATISTICS

Some 2 million Sudanese people were killed during Sudan's second civil war. A further 4 million or more people were displaced or became **refugees** in neighboring countries.

In 2005, Dinka herdsmen and other southern refugees began to return to the homes from which they had fled during the war.

Peace at Last

On January 9, 2005, the Sudanese government and the Sudan People's Liberation Army (SPLA) signed the **Comprehensive Peace Agreement** (CPA) in Nairobi, Kenya. This agreement followed three years of attempted **ceasefires** and peace talks between the north and south. The agreement called for sharing income from oil, and for greater independence for the south. A public vote will take place for southern independence in 2011.

HOT SPOT BRIEFING

FAMINE IN SUDAN
Sudan often suffers from drought conditions, when there is no rain. Food can become extremely scarce, leading to months of famine. Famine in March 2001 affected 3 million Sudanese people.

In January 2005, John Garang (right) shakes hands with Sudan's Vice President Taha, as Omar al-Bashir looks on. They are holding copies of the peace agreement.

VIOLENCE IN DARFUR

Early in 2003, trouble began in the Darfur region of western Sudan. Two Darfur rebel groups, the Justice and Equality Movement (JEM) and the Sudan Liberation Army (SLA), protested to the government in the north about the rights of the people of Darfur.

Conflict Again

At this time, peace was getting closer in the north–south conflict. It was a different matter in western Sudan, though. Fierce fighting broke out. The Darfur rebels fought from four-wheel drive vehicles. They made many successful quick-fire attacks against armed government forces.

HOT SPOT BRIEFING

DIFFERENCES IN DARFUR
The people of Darfur are Muslim, but unlike the people in the north, they are not Arabs. These western Sudanese people felt that the government was ignoring and oppressing black Africans, in favour of Arab people in the north. Their religions were the same, but their languages and cultures were very different.

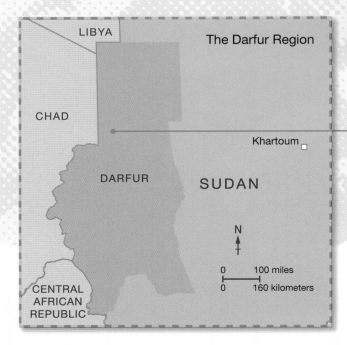

Darfur is an area roughly the size of France, with a population of around 6 million. It is located close to Sudan's border with Chad.

Government Response

In January 2004, the Sudanese government army stopped a revolt by rebels in Darfur. A local armed Arab **militia**, known as the Janjaweed, attacked several villages. Its members killed many people suspected of supporting the Darfur rebel groups. The Janjaweed murdered hundreds of innocent people.

Rebels from the Justice and Equality Movement race across the desert in northern Darfur.

REIGN OF TERROR

In 2003, the **United Nations (UN)** alerted the world to the violent murders in many of Darfur's villages. People were being butchered by the Janjaweed and government forces. By 2004, the UN was calling the situation in Darfur "the world's worst **humanitarian crisis.**"

Deliberate Killings

By the middle of 2004, the United States stated clearly that **genocide** was taking place in Darfur. The Janjaweed and government forces were wiping out groups of black Africans, by murdering them or forcing them to leave the region for ever.

Air Raids

In many attacks, government aircraft first bombed the villages. Then the Janjaweed militia destroyed everything that black Africans could live on. By early 2005, more than 2 million people had fled from their homes in Darfur.

> "Now the village is empty and secure for you. Any village you pass through you must burn."
>
> An unidentified pilot, speaking to a Sudanese army commander in 2004.

Flames rise from a Darfur village in November 2005, after an attack by government-backed militia.

Refugee Camps

Villagers had lost their homes and their possessions. Many had seen their friends and family members murdered. Most survivors became refugees, who had to struggle to reach overcrowded and unhealthy **refugee camps**. Aid workers often tried to reach refugee camps to help Darfuri refugees, but they found it very difficult in this war-torn region. Some were shot at as they tried to bring food and water.

DEATHS IN DARFUR

STATISTICS

Since 2003, there have been at least 200,000 deaths in Darfur due to the conflict. More than 2 million people fled to refugee camps in Sudan. A further 200,000 fled over the border to safety in neighboring Chad.

The Treguine refugee camp in eastern Chad was set up in 2004 for Sudanese families fleeing from Darfur. In 2007, around 15,000 people were living there.

PROSPECTS FOR PEACE

In July 2007, the United Nations Security Council voted to send peacekeeping troops to Darfur. Before this, the only peacekeepers allowed into Darfur were African Union (AU) soldiers. This African organization's aim is to promote peace in the region, but it had only 7,000 soldiers in Darfur.

Larger Force for Peace

The Sudanese government has agreed to accept a larger force of peacekeepers in Darfur. This is a combined force of UN and African Union peacekeepers. Currently there are 9,000 troops based in the area, but this could rise to a possible 26,000 by the beginning of 2009.

"I would like the international force to come so we can go back to farm our land and so our children can go back to school."

Khadija, a refugee in Abu Shouk refugee camp, northern Darfur (reported on a BBC website in October 2007).

An African Union soldier rescues an injured woman after an attack by the Janjaweed.

Need for Agreement

The 2005 peace agreement between northern and southern Sudan brought an end to twenty-one years of civil war. Peace in Darfur seems a very long way off. However, President Bashir has agreed to support the peacekeeping mission and to attend peace talks in Libya in October 2008.

Sudanese women line up for for their daily food rations at a refugee camp in Chad. Hundreds of thousands of refugees from Darfur still rely on food aid from other countries.

FACTFINDER

GEOGRAPHY

Capital Khartoum

Area 967,499 square miles
(2,505,810 square kilometers)

Main rivers Nile

Climate Tropical in the south. Arid desert in the north. Rainy season varies by region (April to November)

Land use   Farmland 7%

Other 93%

PEOPLE

Population 39,379,358

Rate of population change +2.1% per year

Life expectancy 49 years

Average age 18.7 years

Religions   Muslim 70% (mostly in the north)

Christian 5% (mostly in the south and Khartoum)

Native African beliefs 25%

Ethnic groups   Black 52%

Arab 39%

Beja 6%

Other 3%

Literacy   Men 72%

Women 51%

* Gross Domestic Product, or GDP, per person is the total value of all the goods and services produced by a country in a year divided by the number of people in the country. (Source for statistics: *CIA World Factbook,* 2008)

THE ECONOMY

Agricultural products Cotton, peanuts, sorghum, millet, wheat, gum arabic, sugar cane, cassava, mangos, papaya, bananas, sweet potatoes, sesame, sheep, other livestock

Industries Oil, cotton, textiles, cement, edible oils, sugar, soap, distilling, shoes, petroleum products, pharmaceuticals, armaments (weapons), vehicle assembly

Main exports Oil and petroleum products, cotton, sesame, livestock, peanuts, gum arabic, sugar

Gross Domestic Product* $2,500 per person

National earning by sector   Agriculture 31%

Industry 36%

Services 33%

The flag of Sudan

GLOSSARY

al-Qaeda major Islamic terrorist group

capital city city where the government of a region or country is based

ceasefire temporary end to fighting

civilian non-military (civilians are people who are not soldiers)

civil servant government worker

civil war war between different groups in the same country

Comprehensive Peace Agreement final and all-inclusive treaty, or pact, for peace

constitution document stating how a country or state is going to be run

culture things that make a group of people distinctive, such as their language, clothes, food, music, songs, and stories

disarm remove weapons

drought unusually long period with very little rainfall

extremist people whose beliefs go much further than those of ordinary people

famine period when huge numbers of people do not have enough to eat

genocide deliberately killing a nationality or particular group of people

haven shelter or refuge

humanitarian showing concern for others, charitable, or to do with human rights

militia body of unofficial, not professional, soldiers

missionaries people sent on a mission, often to persuade or convert others to a particular religion or cause

Muslim follower of Islam, one of the world's major religions

mutiny rebellion

oppressing keeping down by use of force

parliament group of members or representatives of a political nation

prophet someone who is divinely inspired, or speaks for his god

protocol draft treaty or agreement

refugee camps places where people who have been forced to leave their homes go to live

refugees people forced to leave their homes, usually by fighting

sanctions special restrictions or penalties threatened or carried out as a punishment

terrorist person or people using violence to scare others

United Nations organization set up after World War II that aims to help countries end disputes without fighting

INDEX